Life Untangled:
Living Better
by
Living Easier

Life Untangled:
Living Better
by
Living Easier

Diane E. Dunn

THREE SKILLET

LIFE UNTANGLED: LIVING BETTER BY LIVING EASIER,
Dunn, Diane E.
1st ed.

Books by Diane Dunn:
Organizing Your Home Office for a More Successful You
Life Untangled: Living Better by Living Easier

Diane's books are available from Three Skillet Publishing, Amazon, and from Diane at her website, www.dianedunn.org.

———————

———————

♦♦♦ THREE SKILLET
www.ThreeSkilletPublishing.com

ISBN: 978-1-943189-58-8

A Note from Diane

In my first book, *Organizing Your Home Office for a More Successful You*, my ideas came from my life experience, first as a teenager working in the local mall to managing the front desk of an international business. The response has been overwhelming, and I've returned to an idea I've toyed with for many years.

I'm always receiving tidbits of casual advice on the best way to do things. Some of them I try out, and others I let slip by until I've already wasted part of my day, all because I didn't write down the advice. Other bits of wisdom I've collected on my own as a woman, a businessperson, and a wife and mother. I've thought many times that if I could share my discoveries with others, wouldn't it be great for them to be able to live a better, less tangled life, without the painful learning process I endured?

This book is filled with years of life's hacks and shortcuts, many of which I've used to my advantage. Some of these you'll have seen before and others you may not. I've collected over 350 snippets of wisdom and advice sorted across 18 topics, from Working Outside the Home, to Where Are Your Manners, to Life in the Kitchen.

Each person's circumstances in life are different, and you'll face things that haven't come my way. I've included a section in the back of this book for you to log your own helpful hints to untangling life. I also have a page on my website for even more helpful hints to help make life easier. If you have helpful hints you wish to share with others, email me at helpfulhints@dianedunn.org. I'll post your hints (and even give you credit!) so that others can discover an untangled and stress-free life by following your advice.

I would also love to hear which of my hints you find most useful. Please email me today. Remember, helpfulhints@dianedunn.org. I'm looking forward to hearing from you soon!

Sincerely,
Diane Dunn
www.dianedunn.org

Table of Contents

At Home in Your Home Office

~ 1 Corinthians 13:13 ~

*So now faith, hope, and love abide, these three;
but the greatest of these is love.*

Home Office
Helpful Hints

Always keep your glass in the same location on your desk to avoid accidental spills.

Color Coding for your files: Red – Personal; Blue – Medical; Yellow – Home; Green – Financial; Orange – Insurance

Create a mail station.

Have a file folder or cubby for every member of the household.

Sort incoming mail.

Shred all non-essential mail.

Keep your business cards updated.

Keep your In-Box Tray empty. Letting it overflow is distracting.

Keep a lint roller at work for unexpected dust you may encounter.

Always keep an umbrella in your office for the unexpected storm.

Be professional when in a business situation.

Pay attention to detail.

Help others rise to their potential.

Do your research; if you do not know how, Google it. Research, research, research.

Always follow through with your promises to family or business associates.

Get dressed for work before going to your home office.

Use a dedicated phone for your business and answer it professionally.

Cleaning Up, Cleaning Out

~ 1 John 4:19 ~

We love because he first loved us.

Cleaning Up

Helpful Hints

Magic erasers clean your sink and bathtub without much effort. When finished cleaning, toss it into the washer (but NOT in dryer).

When cleaning out items in your home, take a picture of those you want to remember.

When clearing out a child's room, help them photograph the toys to ease the transition. It will provide a good memory.

Clean the dryer lint screen after every use to lower the risk of the dryer catching fire.

Remember to dust the inside of your cabinets and drawers.

After every use of a lint roller, dispose of the used sheet so it is ready for you the next time you need it.

Label makers are handy in a home office, pantry, laundry, and garage.

When storing boxes in the garage or shed, seal all openings with packing tape.

When purchasing packing tape, choose a brand with high quality ratings as the tape will adhere longer.

For storing brooms, mops, and umbrellas, use a utility rack. This is great for the garage, laundry room or closet.

Keep your jewelry clean with sonic washers or jewelry-cleaning brushes.

Deep in Conversation

~ 1 Peter 4:8 ~

*Above all, keep loving one another earnestly,
since love covers a multitude of sins.*

Conversation
Helpful Hints

Limit your storytelling to three to four minutes.

When you give your word . . . keep it!

Avoid answering a call while engaged in conversation.

Refrain from giving unsolicited advice to others.

Never finish another person's sentence.

Be friendly.

Ask questions and pay attention to the answers.

Know when the conversation is ending and break it off.

Dining Out

*And I commend joy, for man has no good thing
under the sun but to eat and drink and be
joyful . . .*

Dining Out

Helpful Hints

Do not stack plates for the waitstaff.

Always ask your server their name and use it during the meal.

Leave an appropriate tip.

Mind your manners and do not clank your silverware on the inside of a glass while stirring your drink. (Yes, this is possible.)

When cutting your meat, only cut one bite at a time. Adults do not need a pile of cut-up meat on their plates.

Cut your bites small enough so that if you are asked a question, they can be swallowed quickly.

Eat at the speed of others at the table.

Always leave a little food on your plate.

Before beginning to eat, wait for everyone to be served.

Refrain from glancing at your phone during a meal.

Use an orange slice in your iced tea or iced water for a hint of sweetness.

Your drink is to be on your right.

Place a small amount of butter on the bread plate and butter your bread one bite at a time.

Chew with your mouth closed.

When one eats alone, table manners can become relaxed. Always sit up straight and use proper manners while dining, even alone.

Always begin your meal with the fork on the outside.

When dining out as a guest, never order anything more expensive than your host has ordered.

When sharing a meal, ask for a separate plate.

Most restaurants will provide a to-go bag for uneaten food.

Thank the hostess on the way out.

Everything Personal

~ Psalm 118:5 ~

Out of my distress I called on the Lord; the Lord answered me and set me free.

Personal
Helpful Hints

Make your bed every morning.

Your body language speaks volumes about you.

Learn from your mistakes so you do not repeat them.

Be confident.

Don't be a time waster.

Be mindful of the tone of your voice.

Focus on your goals.

Always carry a variety of bills (cash) for tips.

Be punctual.

Never chew gum at an event or meeting.

Never depart without saying goodbye.

Ask for permission before sharing anyone's information on social media (good or bad).

You will learn much by listening and not speaking.

Arrive 10 minutes prior to the scheduled time.

Never criticize or complain.

Look for solutions, not excuses.

Everything has a place; always return the item to where it belongs.

Listen and pay attention to the person
speaking to you.

Never cough or sneeze on someone.

Be honest.

Keep your jewelry and watches clean.

Never tap your fingers while in public.

Use good posture.

Live your life as an example.

Never compromise your values or beliefs.

Be truthful.

Learn to read body language.

Always stand tall with your shoulders back.

Create a morning routine.

Educate yourself on many topics.

Create a plan for success.

Read your written goals daily.

Don't make excuses.

Create a goal card and use it.

Be open to change.

Avoid getting angry.

Make a good first impression.

Exercise at least ten minutes a day.

Humans at Large

*Be kind to one another, tenderhearted, forgiving
one another, as God in Christ forgave you.*

Around People

Helpful Hints

Associate with positive people.

Clean up after yourself.

Don't monopolize others' time.

If you find yourself in a hurry, make a point to leave earlier.

Never hurt another person's feelings.

Zero in on solutions, not problems.

Focus on the positive in everyone.

Relationships require the participation of all parties.

Smiles are contagious.

Find the balance between working and living life.

Don't compare your life to others. You are unique.

Be encouraging to others.

Surround yourself with positive influences.

Don't walk away from a challenge.

Eat healthy meals.

Drink plenty of water.

Learn from your mistakes and stop looking in the rearview mirror.

Keep a record of the good things that happen to you.

Every day find something to be grateful for . . . and write it down!

Count your blessings . . . seriously!

Hygiene In and Out of the Home

~ Ecclesiastes 12:13 ~

The end of the matter; all has been heard. Fear God and keep his commandments, for this is the whole duty of man.

Hygiene

Helpful Hints

When dining at home, keep your hands clean
while preparing food.

Picking your teeth in public is bad manners.

Be mindful of the different scents you may be wearing at one time (hand lotion, makeup, cologne, perfume, hair spray, body wash).

When your nail trimmers are not trimming as easily as they should, replace them.

Remember to clean your belly button and behind your ears when bathing.

Keep your hairbrush and comb clean.

When packing your lunch, add baby wipes to clean your hands before eating.

Always wash your hands thoroughly with soap and warm water after using the restroom.

In and Out of Your Vehicle

~ 1 Chronicles 16:11 ~

Seek the Lord and his strength; seek his presence continually!

Your Vehicle

Helpful Hints

Be a polite driver.

Keep your vehicle clean inside and out.

Maintain every part of your vehicle.

The cleanliness of your vehicle speaks
volumes about who you are.

Always keep an umbrella in your vehicle for
that unexpected storm.

Pull into a parking space so it appears you want to be there.

Always park within the boundaries of your parking space.

Learn the proper way to enter and exit a vehicle.

Keep disposable gloves in your trunk so your hands stay clean when you are pumping gas.

Keep baby wipes in the glove compartment or console.

You may want to keep a travel-size lint roller in your vehicle.

Keep a hand towel in your vehicle for those unexpected spills.

Your hand towel will come in useful as a bib or to lay in your lap while eating in your vehicle.

Your trunk is not a second closet. Empty it every time you arrive home.

If your car interior smells, place an apple under your seat for a day before removing it.

For interior freshness, lay a dryer sheet under the seat. Replace weekly.

Travel tissues are a driver's best friend.

Life in the Kitchen

Therefore I tell you, do not be anxious about . . .
what you will eat or what you will drink . . . Is
not life more than food, and the body more than
clothing?

Kitchen

Helpful Hints

Keep an open container of baking soda in your fridge and freezer for freshness. Change it every 30 days.

Clean your cutting boards with salt or baking soda. Wash with soap and water afterward.

Parchment paper is great for lining metal pans.

Always wear a chef's apron.

Use fresh cooking oil.

When deep frying, use long-handled tongs to place the food into the hot grease.

Wear an oven mitt when placing food into hot grease to protect your hand and arm from grease spatters.

Clean as you cook.

Never pre-slice a cake more than 15-20 minutes before serving to keep it moist.

Keep your knives clean and sharpened.

Read the entire recipe before you begin to prepare it.

Always measure the ingredients exactly.

Roll your cookie dough into bite-size balls before cooking.

Chill cookie dough for 30 minutes to an hour before baking.

Use a cake tester for the cakes and breads
you have prepared.

Before cooking your meatloaf, stew, or soup,
slice and chop all ingredients.

Before preparing a recipe, gather all the
ingredients to insure you have what you
need.

Spread the mayo on your sandwich to cover the entire slice of bread.

Check the safety seal on a product to ensure it hasn't been tampered with.

Clean burnt pans with tomato paste, sauce or ketchup before washing with soap and water.

Never try a new recipe for the first time for a special event.

Keep all sharp kitchen utensils in one drawer.

Place your sponge in the silverware tray of the dishwasher with every wash.

Baking stones are great for baking, and the clean-up is easy.

Never place oil or butter in the water while cooking your pasta, as the sauce will not adhere to the pasta.

Never rinse your pasta after cooking it.

Keep the handles of your pans turned inward to avoid knocking them off the stove.

When entertaining, reserve the salad ingredients for the guests to add to their bed of lettuce.

Label the shelves in your pantry.

In your pantry or cabinet, store all baking items (food and specialty utensils) together.

Arrange spices alphabetically.

Designate specific areas in your pantry for items.

Transfer your dry goods to freezer zipper bags then place each bag into the original box.

When purchasing rice, place 2 cups of rice into freezer or storage zipper bags and drop the bags back into the original boxes.

Store dry goods in plastic containers in the pantry.

Use turntables in the corners of the pantry and all kitchen cabinets.

Create a separate section in the pantry for non-food items.

Cover your pot when bringing water to a boil to speed up the process.

When slicing juicy items, place a large piece of foil under your food and fold up the edges.

Place a paper towel under your cutting board to assist you in catching residual juice for an easy clean up.

When the food you are baking in the oven catches fire, do not open the oven door. The fire will extinguish itself.

Store extra food in freezer zip lock bags.

Always rinse the dish rag after every use before placing it to rest on the sink, so that it is clean for the next use.

If you have a trash can and it's difficult to remove the bag, insert an extra bag in the can and your trash will slide right out.

Store spices in a cool and dark place, not above your stove.

Taste what you have prepared before serving it.

If storing perishables, remove them from their plastic store-issue bags.

Store larger boxes on their side in the pantry.

If removing food from its original container, identify the expiration date on its new container.

Wash and dry your hands before food preparation.

Keep cabinet doors and drawers closed to keep from bumping into them.

Wipe up spills immediately.

Before exiting the kitchen, make sure the stove and oven are off.

Keep paper and cloth products away from
the burners.

Never put water on a cooking fire.

Always set the timer to avoid burning food.

Living with Children

~ Philippians 1:6 ~

*And I am sure of this, that he who began a good
work in you will bring it to completion at the
day of Jesus Christ.*

Children

Helpful Hints

Children will watch and memorize your every action.

Teach your children etiquette from an early age.

Introduce proper table manners to your children as soon as they can eat independently.

When packing lunches, add durable but disposable plates, flatware, and cloth napkins when possible, for a pleasant experience.

Teach your children to be confident in who they are.

Keep a calendar where your children can see all scheduled family activities.

Encourage your children to be responsible.

Encourage your children to work independently.

Monitor homework.

Teach your children proper kitchen
techniques.

Be consistent in the words and examples you
show your children.

Always carry a supply of healthy snacks.

Raise your children to respect others and the world around them.

Encourage your children to read.

Off the Clothing Rack

~ Philippians 4:4 ~

Rejoice in the Lord always; again I will say, Rejoice.

Clothing

Helpful Hints

Keep your clothes and accessories pristine.

Dress appropriately for each occasion.

Keep your shoes brushed or polished.

If showing signs of wear, shoes need to be repaired or replaced.

Take a few minutes to sew on that missing button.

Never wear a neck tie with spots or fraying thread.

Always wear clean clothes.

Don't over accessorize.

Keep your clothes classy and tasteful.

Wear panty hose (women) with your dresses to work.

Keep a safety pin with you at all times for emergency clothing repair.

Provocative clothing is inappropriate in a work environment.

Use panty liners to protect the underarms of your garments from perspiration (men, too!).

Wear properly fitting clothes.

Open-toed shoes are for casual wear, not work.

Your belt, shoes, and hand bag (or wallet) should match.

A good clothes brush helps keep you pristine all day.

Shopping at the Market

~ Proverbs 10:22 ~

The blessing of the Lord makes rich, and he adds no sorrow with it.

Market

Helpful Hints

The butcher usually has recipes and cooking instructions for the meat you are purchasing.

Stop at the meat counter last of all while shopping.

At the meat counter, if a package is not cold to the touch, do not purchase that item.

While grocery shopping, always reach to the back for your items. They will be fresher.

Always check the expiration dates on all packages of food before purchasing.

While grocery shopping, place raw meat, chicken and fish into individual plastic store-supplied bags.

Always spend the extra time to shop for the freshest ingredients.

Shop online, if your local market offers this service, to save time and money and avoid impulse purchases.

Be observant of your surroundings in the parking lot. Not everyone wishes you well.

Compare unit prices, not just the package price.

Remember to remove the attached coupon to get credit at checkout.

Stay within your shopping budget or allowance.

Check circulars if your store price matches.

Make a list and stick to it.

The upper and lower shelves usually hold the less expensive products.

Do you really need that last-minute add on item at the cash register?

Sign up for the rewards club, if your store has one.

Speech Heard Around the World

~ Psalm 23:1 ~

A Psalm of David. The Lord is my shepherd; I shall not want.

Speech

Helpful Hints

Curse words are inappropriate for any conversation.

Learn a new word every day.

Interrupting someone while they are speaking is rude.

Enunciate your words when speaking.

Improve your speech with lessons, if necessary.

Always greet someone with, "Hello."

Use a thesaurus to enhance your vocabulary.

Adapt the volume of your voice to your surroundings.

Pay attention to the person with whom you are speaking.

Keep your speeches short and clear.

Watch your words while in public. You never know who is listening.

Surfing the Internet and Social Media

~ Psalm 46:10 ~

Be still, and know that I am God. I will be exalted among the nations, I will be exalted in the earth!

Internet

Helpful Hints

Be careful of the words and photos you post on social media. They will be out there forever, even if you delete them.

Proof your messages before pressing the send button.

Reply to emails within 24 hours.

Include a signature in all emails.

Begin your email with a proper greeting and
end your email with a proper closing.

Keep your website up to date.

Never discuss confidential information via email or social media messaging.

When searching online, it's not necessary to type http:// or www.

Open the desired web page in a new tab by right-clicking with your mouse and choosing *Open in a New Tab.*

Have a reliable security program on your computer.

Ask Google anything.

Teach your children about privacy and
security while online.

Verify the sites you visit are safe by checking
in the address bar for the green, locked
security symbol.

Always close the browser window when
exiting a site that requires a password.

Taking Care of
Business

~ Hebrews 11:1 ~

*Now faith is the assurance of things hoped for,
the conviction of things not seen.*

Business

Helpful Hints

When departing from a business meeting, say, "It was a pleasure meeting with you and thank you for your time."

When being introduced to someone, repeat their name as you hear it and use it in a sentence during the conversation.

End conversations by saying, "Paul, it was a pleasure meeting you." Be sure to use their name.

Name tags should be worn on your right side.

Create a plan and follow it.

Always be willing to assist.

Remain professional in a business
environment.

Avoid social media sites while at work.

Keep a sense of humor about work situations.

Set an example for others to follow.

Always use a back-up service for your computer.

Keep an encrypted password list.

Be cooperative and supportive, even when you don't feel like it.

Always use a calendar. Never assume you will remember every meeting or appointment.

Use proper posture to avoid neck and back strain.

Stand up every hour and stretch.

Maintain a well-balanced and comfortable temperature in your office.

Be willing to go the extra mile.

Reduce overexposure to your monitor and/or screen to reduce eyestrain.

Schedule breaks away from your workstation/office.

Be committed to excellence.

Consider all options before forming an opinion.

Once you've formed an opinion, keep it to yourself.

Using Your Phone

~ Psalm 146:2 ~

I will praise the Lord as long as I live; I will sing praises to my God while I have my being.

Phone

Helpful Hints

Identify yourself immediately when calling
someone on the phone.

There is no need to shout while speaking on a
mobile phone.

When giving out your phone number, speak slowly and give your number in this pattern: three digits, three digits, and four digits.

When leaving a voice mail make the message short and to the point. Leave your phone number twice.

With every phone call you make, be prepared to leave a message.

Only use speaker phone mode when in private.

Never hang up on anyone. State that you are going to hang up, then say goodbye before ending the call.

Blue tooth earpieces should only be worn while you are engaged in a phone conversation.

145

Refrain from answering your phone while in a public restroom.

When calling someone, be sure and ask if you have called at a good time.

Refrain from looking at your phone while in a conversation.

Never answer the phone while chewing gum.

Never answer the phone with a mint in your mouth.

When speaking on the phone, smile while talking. It will change the tone of your voice.

Disable background data for nonessential apps.

Secure your device with a password.

Use your phone as a wireless hot spot for only a small charge each month.

Extend your battery by turning on your phone's low power mode.

Use the Remind Me Later feature to skip calls on the iPhone.

Use a cloud service to share photos with your friends.

Carry a portable battery pack for emergency charging.

Back up your data to avoid losing important information, pictures and videos.

While traveling, use the USB port on the back of hotel televisions to charge your phone.

Using Wi-Fi will cut down on data usage and the extra cost it can incur.

Disable notifications and turn the Fetch function off.

The panorama camera feature can capture everything around you.

Use the Disk Usage app to identify excess data usage.

Use your camera to remember signs, ads, and reminders, and take screenshots of coupons.

Only download approved apps.

Where Are Your Manners

Whatever you do, work heartily, as for the Lord and not for men.

Manners

Helpful Hints

In correspondence, respond to RSVPs
immediately.

Manners matter. Be mannerly in all
situations.

Remember to say, "Thank you."

Remember to say, "Please."

Be very careful of your words.

Laugh softly in the presence of others.

Remember to say, "I apologize," not, "I'm sorry."

Never correct someone while they are speaking.

Chewing ice in the presence of others is rude.

Offer genuine compliments to others, as it will make their day.

Only speak positively about what you see.

Be polite.

Respect personal space (usually an arm's length).

Never give out someone's personal information without permission.

Always write a thank you note and mail it.

Keep thank you notes simple. Acknowledge the gift, express how it made you feel, and say thank you.

Never speak with food in your mouth.

Remove your gloves upon entering a building.

Wipe your feet before entering a home.

Always thank military personnel for serving.

Do not be critical of others.

Do not pop your chewing gum.

Watch your actions while in public; there are cameras everywhere.

When in error, apologize quickly.

Pets are not always welcome.

Make others feel comfortable.

Greet everyone with a smile.

Help someone put on their coat if they are struggling.

Always say, "Excuse me," when exiting from your location.

After being introduced to someone, before you leave, say, "It was a pleasure to have met you."

Show respect to others.

Use a tissue when you sneeze.

Your Helpful Hints
(Feel free to be as creative as you wish!)

~ Proverbs 16:9 ~

The heart of man plans his way, but the Lord establishes his steps.

Your

Helpful Hints

_____

_____

_____

_____

_____

_____

— Space for Your Helpful Hints —

_____

_____

_____

_____

_____

_____

_____

_____

_____

_____

_____

_____

— Space for Your Helpful Hints —

— Space for Your Helpful Hints —

_____

_____

_____

_____

_____

_____

_____

_____

_____

_____

_____

_____

— Space for Your Helpful Hints —

— Space for Your Helpful Hints —

_____

_____

_____

_____

_____

_____

_____

_____

_____

_____

_____

_____

— Space for Your Helpful Hints —

— Space for Your Helpful Hints —

_____

_____

_____

_____

_____

_____

_____

_____

_____

_____

_____

_____

_____

_____

_____

_____

_____

_____

_____

_____

_____

_____

_____

_____

— Space for Your Helpful Hints —

_____

_____

_____

_____

_____

_____

_____

_____

_____

_____

_____

_____

_____

_____

_____

_____

_____

_____

_____

_____

_____

_____

_____

— Space for Your Helpful Hints —

— More Space for Your Helpful Hints —

— More Space for Your Helpful Hints —

— More Space for Your Helpful Hints —

www.ingramcontent.com/pod-product-compliance
Lightning Source LLC
Chambersburg PA
CBHW060923040426
42445CB00011B/766